W9-BEP-482

LIFE DURING THE GREAT CIVILIZATIONS

The Maya

**Charles George
and Linda George**

**BLACKBIRCH®
PRESS**

THOMSON
—★—
GALE

San Diego • Detroit • New York • San Francisco • Cleveland • New Haven, Conn. • Waterville, Maine • London • Munich

LIBRARY OF CONGRESS CATALOGING-IN-PUBLICATION DATA

George, Charles, 1949-
  Maya / by Charles and Linda George.
    p. cm. — (Life during the great civilizations)
Includes bibliographical references and index.
Contents: Mayan society — Daily life — Science and technology — One God or many?
  ISBN 1-56711-738-4 (hardback : alk. paper)
  1. Mayas—History—Juvenile literature. 2. Mayas—Social life and customs—Juvenile literature. [1. Mayas. 2. Indians of Central America.] I. George, Linda. II. Title. III. Series.

  F1435.G42 2004
  972.81'016—dc22   2003013003

Printed in United States
10 9 8 7 6 5 4 3 2 1

Contents

The Mayan World

Centuries before the arrival of Europeans to the New World, a mysterious race of Indians built a highly advanced civilization on the Yucatán Peninsula in southern Mexico and Central America. Evidence of that civilization—sculpture and pottery unearthed in ancient cities, an amazingly accurate calendar, and a complex system of hieroglyphic writing—has led researchers to compare Mayan civilization to those of Egypt, Greece, and Rome. This advanced American culture belonged to the people called the Maya. It is not known what they called themselves.

The Mystery of the Maya

When Spanish conquistadors landed on the gulf coast of the Yucatán Peninsula in the sixteenth century, they were baffled to find natives living in primitive grass huts near the ruins of breathtakingly beautiful cities. These magnificent cities had contained pyramids, temples, astronomical observatories, and hundreds of other impressive structures, but the natives the conquistadors encountered seemed to know nothing of their history. Apparently, the grand civilization that had risen at some time in the past from simple farming villages and create those cities had, by the 1500s, fallen back into an agrarian culture.

Explorers and scientists have debated for centuries what happened to the Maya. No one knew for sure why such an advanced civilization had fallen. Some thought an epidemic had

Opposite Page: The pyramid in Chichen Itza (pictured) and other Mayan structures intrigued the Spanish conquistadors who arrived on the Yucatán Peninsula in the 1500s.

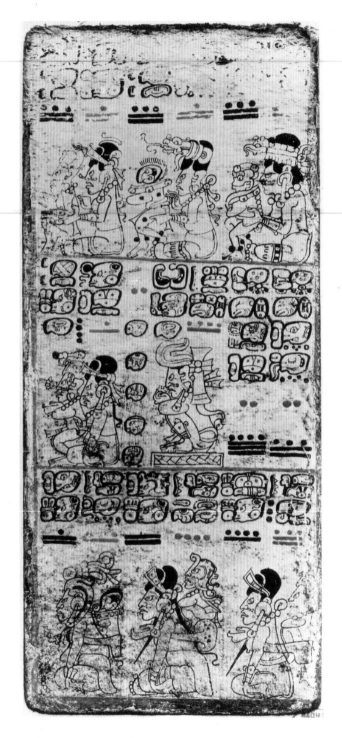

wiped out most of the population. Others believed a peasant revolt had overthrown the Mayan kings. Still others believed the Maya exhausted the soil, causing food shortages and famine. More recently, scientists believe a combination of factors led to the fall of the Mayan Empire—including war between Maya city-states, overpopulation, and crop failures

Scientists have studied archaeological evidence, but written records would yield more specific information. Until recently, the Mayan hieroglyphic language had not been translated. In addition, despite the fact that the Maya produced extensive written records, only a few remain. Parts of their story come from the few documents that survived, works written by Mayan authors either before the Spanish arrived or after the conquest. Most other Mayan literature was destroyed. The *Dresden Codex*, one of only three existing preconquest documents, is a volume about Mayan astronomy and fortune telling. *Popol Vuh*, an epic poem, was a sacred book written just a few years after the Spanish arrived. Finally, the books of *Chilam Balam*,

compiled by Mayan writers between the sixteenth and eighteenth centuries, contain folklore and information about astrology and medicine, along with a few historical stories. These books were found and preserved by Spanish conquistadors when they arrived in the sixteenth century. Most other Mayan literature was destroyed.

The most important sources of Mayan history, however, are the writings of Antonio de Ciudad-Real and Diego de Landa, Christian priests sent to Yucatán by Spain. Almost all of what is known of the Maya living at the time of the Spanish conquest, and, by inference, of those living centuries before, comes from the writings, or relaci"nes, of these friars. De Landa's small book, *Relación de las Cosas de Yucatán*, written in 1566, is today one of the principal sources of late Mayan history. However, these stories were written by Christian men about pagan people, and they are, in places, somewhat biased.

Today, more is being learned about the Maya through the translation of hieroglyphic carvings in cities such as Bonampak, Copán, Palenque, and Chichén Itzá. Also, discoveries of undisturbed Mayan tombs have answered questions that have intrigued archaeologists for decades. Piece by piece, the story of the Maya continues to emerge.

With the translation of hieroglyphic carvings (pictured), archaeologists have learned more about politics, economics, and religion in Mayan society.

Opposite Page: The Dresden Codex (pictured), a Mayan document, gave archaeologists insight into Mayan astronomy and fortune-telling.

CHAPTER ONE

Mayan Society

The Maya never united into one central empire. Instead, their society was organized into city-states similar to those of ancient Greece. Each city, and the land immediately surrounding it, had its own government, controlled by a king, priests, and a noble class. So far, dozens of major cities as well as hundreds of other minor sites have been discovered. There was apparently a good deal of rivalry between individual city-states.

In the ruins of the Mayan city Bonampak, ornate murals inside the tomb of a Mayan king paint a vivid picture of life during the classic period of Mayan civilization (A.D. 250 to A.D. 900), the period during which the Maya made their greatest achievements. In these murals, Mayan society is portrayed as having strict social classes with kings at the top; priests, nobles, warriors, and artisans slightly lower in rank; common people below that; and slaves at the lowest level.

Social Classes

In Mayan society, there were two basic classes of people; the elite, or *ah mehenob*, "higher men"; and the common people, or *yalba uinicob*, "lower men." Within the *ah mehenob*, there were several subdivisions. Kings of the various Mayan city-states were few in number and occupied the highest level of society. Below them were priests, called *ahkinob* in the Mayan language. Beneath the priest class were nobles, wealthy

Opposite Page: This image from a fresco found at the Mayan city Bonampak shows warriors as they capture prisoners. Warriors were members of the nobility.

landowners called *uytzam chinamital*, professional warriors known as *achij*, and merchants, or *ahbeyom*.

Commoners, the largest group, occupied the lower-middle levels of Mayan society, but there were divisions within this group as well, usually related to occupation. Skilled craftsmen were held in higher regard than unskilled laborers. The largest occupational group of Mayan commoners was farmers, but not all farmers owned land. Some were landless peasants who worked land owned by others. The lowest status in Mayan society, as in most civilizations, belonged to slaves.

Mayan Lifestyles

Mayan Kings

Mayan kings were revered as gods. As such, they were not expected to work like common people. Instead, they presided over elite councils

The carving in this stela, or stone pillar, depicts a Mayan king. Such carvings often honored the achievements of kings.

and made decisions that affected the city-state. They lived in lavish palaces and were attended by servants. According to murals in Mayan cities, kings wore elaborate headdresses, capes of brilliantly colored feathers, and intricate jade and shell jewelry. Much is known about Mayan kings because stone pillars, or stela, were carved to commemorate their achievements. Most kings were buried in elaborate tombs that featured colorful murals depicting their lives.

Priests

Priests were second only to the king in power. The high priest in each city-state, the *ah awcan*, or "Lord Serpent," received offerings from the lower priests and nobles. Priests were keepers of the calendar and the sacred chronicles— records of Mayan history and astrological charts.

Their knowledge of astronomy and mathematics allowed them to predict events that would affect Mayan life, such as the beginning of the rainy season and solar and lunar eclipses. They also passed on the history of their people and knowledge of Mayan hieroglyphic writing.

Below the high priests were the *ahkinob*, or "they of the sun," who conducted most day-to-day rituals. All priests lived in or near the temples and wore ornate robes and sometimes masks and headdresses.

Members of the nobility enjoyed privileged lifestyles, held important positions in government, and took part in religious ceremonies like the one depicted in this fresco.

Nobles

Members of the nobility shared the privileged lifestyle of the kings. Nobles occupied administrative posts in the government. One of their duties was to oversee public works, such as the construction of pyramids and roads. They helped plan the projects, arranged for the materials to be used, organized the workforce, and supervised the actual construction. In addition, they also supervised the collection of taxes and tribute, participated in religious ceremonies, and commanded armies.

Their homes, built almost entirely of limestone, were clustered near ceremonial centers. Nobles, too, wore fine robes and jewelry, and many were buried in decorated tombs.

Middle Classes

Those Maya in the middle class were ranked according to their professions. Artisans and craftsmen helped build and decorate monuments to honor their kings. They carved bas-relief sculpture on the walls, painted murals to decorate Mayan tombs, and produced pottery and statues to adorn the structures. Merchants and tradesmen produced the goods each city-state traded with its neighbors.

Clothing worn by the middle class was simpler. Men wore an *ex*, pronounced "eesh," a woven cotton loincloth wrapped around the

Artisans, craftsmen, merchants, and tradesmen made up the Mayan middle class. Men wore an ex, a loincloth worn around the waist, as shown below.

waist and tied between the legs. Middle-class Mayan men wore a garment called a *pati*, similar to a poncho, around their shoulders. Women wore simple clothing, either a cotton dress called a *kub* or *huipel*, or a skirt and another garment wrapped around the chest made from a piece of cloth called a manta. Covering their shoulders was a cotton shawl, or *booch*. Their homes were usually made of limestone, but they were smaller, less ornate, and located farther from the city's center than those of the nobles.

Commoners lived outside the cities in simple thatched-roof huts made of mud, poles, and plaster.

Commoners

Most commoners were either farmers or servants. Farmers lived in simple huts away from the cities. Servants' homes were located closer to the homes of their masters. Most commoners lived in simple huts constructed of poles, mud, and plaster, with high-pitched, thatched roofs.

These huts usually had two rooms, no windows, and one opening with no door. Peasant houses, because of their simple construction, lasted only one generation before being torn down. Each time the resident of a house died, he or she was buried under the floor before the house was destroyed.

Farmers wore simple cotton garments and sandals and raised food for themselves and as tribute—gifts—for the king and nobles. During the dry season, many farmers worked on causeways, temples, and palaces. They also cut wood for fuel and for timber. During times of war, they served as soldiers. Servants, because they worked in their masters' homes, dressed in more ornate clothes.

Slaves

Known as *p'entacob*, most slaves had been captured in war, sentenced as criminals, or were poor individuals who had been sold into slavery. Little is known about their lifestyle, but theirs was not an easy life. They performed the most menial jobs, such as digging trenches and waterways, building dams for reservoirs, and quarrying rocks for building temples.

Slaves wore meager clothing, usually just a loincloth made from coarser material than that worn by commoners higher on the social scale. They also went barefoot. Many times, slaves were sacrificed to the Mayan gods during religious ceremonies or during drought or war. Archaeological evidence suggests that each noble's slaves lived communally, in barracks.

Each class in Mayan society had its own distinct characteristics. Members of one class, in whatever city-state they lived, shared similar lifestyles, homes, and professions, but they were all Maya. Across the Yucatán Peninsula, though, all Maya, no matter their position in society, shared a common ancestry, common physical appearance, and common social customs.

The Maya Today

Many modern-day Maya still wear the simple cotton clothing of their ancestors.

Many of today's Maya live much as their ancestors did before the rise of the classic period of Mayan civilization. In rural areas of Belize, Honduras, Guatemala, and the Mexican state of Chiapas, Mayan farmers still live in thatched-roof houses, wear simple cotton clothes, follow a version of the old Mayan calendar, and grow primarily corn. The Yucatán Maya call themselves *mazehualob* or the common people, though they speak a mixture of Spanish and Mayan. They also practice a unique combination of Christianity and their ancient Mayan religion, including a frequent ceremony honoring Chac, the Mayan god of rain.

Tourism in that part of Mexico and Central America, including the resort areas of Cancún and Cozumel, has brought some changes to the Maya who live in urban areas. Many wear manufactured clothing, work at nontraditional jobs, and speak predominantly Spanish, but at heart, they are still Maya.

CHAPTER TWO

Daily Life

Much has been learned about the lives of Mayan kings, priests, and nobles by observing carvings and murals, and by deciphering Mayan hieroglyphics. The lower classes, however, were seldom represented in Mayan art, and few artifacts belonging to common people have been found.

To learn about the typical Mayan peasant, scientists must rely upon eyewitness reports from visitors such as Diego de Landa and by observing modern Mayan peasants in Mexico and Central America. Many of their practices and customs are identical to those reported by de Landa.

How Did They Look?

In physical appearance, the Maya were short, stocky people, with straight, shiny black hair and skin the color of copper. Their broad faces featured high cheekbones, dark eyes, and prominent noses. In ancient times, a Mayan man wore his hair long, braiding it around his head and leaving a pigtail hanging down the back. The hair was short on top. Facial hair was considered unattractive, so many pulled it out with copper tweezers. Mayan women, too, wore their hair long, and they arranged it in various styles, depending upon whether or not they were married.

Opposite Page: Mayan peasants today have retained the much of the culture, traditions, and appearance of their ancestors.

The Maya considered a dramatically sloping forehead, like that of the official depicted on this Mayan vessel, a feature that denoted nobility.

Tattooing was common among married individuals, and the colors and designs served to identify them as members of a particular social class. Tattoos were pricked into the skin with a sharp bone or a knife made from obsidian, a dark, glassy volcanic rock. Pigment was then rubbed into the wounds. This was extremely painful, so tattoos also represented valor and courage.

Face and body painting were also common. Pigment for the body paint came from plant and mineral sources native to the area. For men, the colors were important. Young unmarried warriors and men who were fasting for religious reasons painted themselves black. Red signified a warrior, and blue was the color of priests and victims of sacrificial rites. Women painted their faces red, but this had no social or religious importance. It was simply a way of protecting them from the sun and insects.

A feature unique to the Maya was a dramatically sloping forehead, but this was not a natural characteristic. It had to be developed over time and gave what the Maya considered to be a noble appearance to the head. Shortly after birth, a Mayan child was placed in a rigid cradle, the head bound between two boards. This procedure flattened the child's head.

Another unusual Mayan practice was an attempt to cross the child's eyes, which was also considered a mark of beauty and distinction. The parents hung a ball in front of the child's face, between the eyes, so close that the eyes naturally began to cross. No record mentions what effect this practice had on their vision.

What Did They Eat?

Although kings and nobles ate more lavishly, even the common Maya ate a balanced diet. Corn, or maize, made up about 50 percent of the daily food intake. Mayan women made tortillas, a type of flat bread commonly used throughout Latin America today. Tortillas were served with every meal, either to scoop food from a bowl or to wrap it in, making what is called today a taco or burrito. Besides this widespread use, the Maya also used cornmeal in nearly everything they ate or drank. Corn provided carbohydrate, beans provided protein, and squash and chili peppers had essential vitamins. With the addition of fresh fruits and some meat, their diet was complete.

On a typical day in a Mayan village, the woman of the house rose before dawn to start the fire. She made the day's supply of tortillas from maize that she and her daughters had ground the night before on

Like their ancestors, these modern-day Mayan women make corn tortillas to serve with every meal.

Popular Beverages

Raising bees allowed the Maya to have abundant amounts of honey. They not only used honey to flavor foods, they fermented it to make an alcoholic beverage. Like the Aztec, the Maya also loved to consume a relatively bitter drink made by mixing ground corn with ground cacao beans. Cacao beans are roasted and ground, then mixed with sweeteners to make chocolate. Cacao was not grown in most areas of the Mayan Empire, so it was rather expensive and highly prized. Cacao beans even served as money.

The Maya made a popular drink from ground cacao beans (pictured) and ground corn.

flat stones called metates. The man of the house departed for the fields about dawn with a lunch consisting of several apple-size balls of ground maize wrapped in leaves and flavored with chili peppers.

Early in the afternoon, the farmer returned home, where his wife had a bath ready for him. He napped during the hottest time of day, often in a hammock outside the hut. When he awoke, the evening meal was ready. Men sat on low wooden stools or woven grass mats and were served by women. A stew of deer meat, fowl, or fish was usually consumed with tortillas. They drank water mixed with cornmeal.

Family Life

Daily life for the Maya was controlled by forces they could not see or understand. They believed the position of the stars, the movements of the planets, and the phases of the moon had power over them. This belief is called astrology.

In the Mayan Empire, people consulted priests to learn the best days to get married, the correct person to marry, when to have children, and what to name them. The birth of a child was a significant event in a Mayan family, and each date foretold the person's attributes—some good, some neutral, and some bad.

A child's given name, or *paal kaba*, was carefully chosen by a priest or shaman. Each child had several names—his *paal kaba*, or given name, his father's and, *naal kaba*, a combination of his mother's and father's family names; and finally an informal nickname, or *coco kaba*. Masculine given names began with "Ah," as in Ah Cuy (Owl), Ah Tok (Flint Knife), and Ah Kukum (Jaguar), and feminine given names began with "Ix."

About the age of four, as a symbol of childhood, girls received a red shell on a string to be tied around their waists and worn until puberty. Similarly, boys had a small white bead fastened to their hair.

Children lived at home until a coming-of-age ceremony. No evidence has been found of formal schools, but boys and girls learned what they needed to know from their parents. When boys reached fourteen and girls twelve, they were considered old enough for marriage and could leave home.

Women gathered and prepared food, wove cloth, collected firewood, and took care of the home.

All Mayan marriages were arranged, either by fathers or by a professional matchmaker, or *ah atanzahob*. After the marriage, the groom lived with and worked for the bride's family for six or seven years. Then he was permitted to build a separate home for his family. Furniture inside a typical two-room Mayan peasant hut included wooden stools and benches and low beds made of tightly woven grass mats.

Women took care of domestic chores such as collecting firewood, gathering and preparing foods, weaving cloth for clothing, and making household containers from pottery, gourds, and other materials. After working on their own farms to raise what their families needed, Mayan men joined work crews to produce surplus food to give to the king and to build or maintain temples, roads, and palaces.

Families made time to attend religious ceremonies, many involving music with drums, flutes, bells, and trumpets. The Maya had no stringed instruments. At these events, the Maya watched dramatic presentations in which actors presented stories from Mayan mythology. Diego de Landa described one such theater in Chichén Itzá· in 1560: "In front of the north stairway, at some distance, there were two small theatres of masonry, with four staircases, and paved on top with stones, on which they presented plays and comedies to divert the people."[1]

There was little leisure time, even for Mayan children. As soon as they were old enough, they joined their parents and put work ahead of play. When they had time, boys played a board game with beans similar to Parcheesi. They also played with hard balls made from the elastic gum of rubber trees, and they ran and chased each other in games of hunter-and-hunted.

In every culture, people's daily lives, whether at work or at play, are influenced by discoveries and advancements made by that culture's scientists. For the Maya, this was especially true. Developments in agriculture, engineering, astronomy, and mathematics made their lives easier in some ways and more complex in others.

CHAPTER THREE

Science and Technology

The most visible achievement of the Maya are the vast cities they left behind. Advances in architecture and building techniques helped them create cities that in some ways rivaled those of ancient Greece and Rome. In addition, there is evidence of other important but less dramatic Mayan inventions and discoveries.

Early in the development of the Mayan culture, the production of surplus food led to an increase in population, which required a more structured society. A surplus of food allowed more free time for other pursuits and provided a more specialized workforce. Small villages grew into cities that were centers of commerce and government, and particular fields of study, such as astronomy, mathematics, literature, and art, grew in importance.

Agriculture

One of the Maya's most important contributions to mankind was the development of what they called *ixim*—maize, or Indian corn. By careful selection, early Mayan farmers chose the best of the wild grass that grew in the region and crossbred it until they developed a plant that produced more seeds than it needed for reproduction. Maize became an important and abundant food source.

Opposite Page: Architectural innovations allowed the Maya to build temples, pyramids, and other structured that rivaled those of ancient Greece and Rome.

The Maya developed maize, or Indian corn, which made up about half of all the food they ate.

Ancestors of the Maya developed other foods, too. From the small, bitter seeds of a lupine plant, they developed many of the types of beans used around the world today. They developed the pumpkin from a small wild squash and took the thick root of a morning glory and transformed it into the sweet potato. Potatoes and tomatoes, both members of the nightshade family native to Central and South America, were also developed into food sources.

The Maya learned that the fibers of the cotton plant, also native to Central and South America, could be spun and woven into cloth well suited for their tropical climate. Tobacco, another member of the nightshade family of plants, was also native to the region. The Maya discovered that the leaves, when dried, could be burned to produce a sweet-smelling smoke. It was originally used in religious ceremonies as an offering to the gods, but was later chopped and smoked in special pipes. The Maya also used many herbs found in the region as medicines, spices for their food, or in religious ceremonies.

Mayan farming techniques began simply. At first, farmers used the slash-and-burn method. Underbrush was chopped down with a stone ax, or bat, and burned, which left cleared land to plow with a fire-hardened digging stick called a *xul*. This method, which is still used in much of the world, depletes the soil after only a few years. When that happens, more land must be cleared.

Increases in population also made it necessary to clear more land and make it more productive. In later years, the Maya developed extensive systems of irrigation and reclaimed swampland for farming by building raised beds on which to grow crops. To improve transportation and communication, the Maya also built raised roads called causeways to connect their cities.

City Life

Cities built by the Maya in both the classic period and the postclassic period (A.D. 909–A.D. 1697) reflect not only their intellect and craftsmanship, but give modern scientists a glimpse of their city life. The size, location, and arrangement of buildings allow scientists to speculate on what life was like in those cities. In Tikal, for example, the largest Mayan city, the central plaza contains two massive pyramid-temples

The arch was an important architectural feature of Mayan building.

facing each other. One rises to a height of 229 feet. Between these huge structures lies a large open courtyard where masses of people witnessed religious ceremonies.

These structures, and hundreds of others in cities such as Palenque, Piedras Negras, Quiriguá, Chichén Itzá, and Copán, not only give hints about daily life for the citizens of those cities, they also reflect two advances in building techniques and architecture similar to those of the Roman Empire—the arch and cement.

One feature common to many Mayan cities is a ceremonial court, which was used as a theater and for a ball game the Maya called *pok-atok*. The game was played with a hard rubber ball in a court with two stone rings suspended vertically on opposite walls. The object of the game was to knock the ball through one of the stone rings. Players wore little protective padding and used only their elbows and hips to hit the ball. A goal was so rare that if a player made one he had the right to demand all the clothing and jewelry from the spectators.

One Mayan pyramid temple, like the one pictured below, reached a height of 229 feet.

In every Mayan city, murals and carvings depict scenes from Mayan life. Alongside these are thousands of smaller carvings that most archaeologists recognize as a form of hieroglyphic writing. However, for decades, no one knew what the Maya had written.

Recording the Past

Recording past events gave the Maya a sense of their history. They recorded major events, dates, and names in a complex system of hieroglyphics that have only recently been deciphered. In addition to carving their records on stone pillars and the walls of their temples, the Maya also created paper and bound their writings into books. At the time of the Spanish conquest in the 1500s, most Mayan cities had libraries where priests consulted historical documents and astronomical charts to foretell the future and to plan future events.

Spanish priests could not read the symbols, so they assumed they must be evil. Under the leadership of Diego de Landa, Spanish conquistadors burned countless documents that described Mayan life and history. The few Mayan books that survived speak more about astronomy and the passage of time than about Mayan history.

Spanish conquistadors destroyed many historical documents, like the codex pictured above, because they assumed the Mayan hieroglyphics were evil.

Maya Astrology

Few ancient civilizations, in the Old World or the New, were more obsessed with the movement of the stars than the Maya. They worked hard to understand the mysteries of time and space, because they believed there was a direct connection between them and what happened in their lives. This obsession led them to study astronomy. In cities throughout the Yucatán, alongside pyramids, ball courts, and temples, the Maya built observatories to study the skies. Without telescopes or computers, they accurately charted the movement of stars and planets.

Using only fixed lines of sight, crossed sticks, and fixed observation points, the Maya calculated the length of a year on Earth to be 365.2420 days, which is remarkably close to the actual figure of 365.2422. They predicted the changing of seasons, the arrival of comets, and the occurrences of solar and lunar eclipses.

Obsessed with Time

Mathematics and astronomy were only tools for the creation of the most important technological advance for the Maya—an accurate calendar. Almost twelve hundred years before the adoption of the calendar used today—the Georgian calendar—the Maya calendar was as precise and as accurate.

The Mayan calendar is actually three separate, overlapping calendars. The Haab calendar, based on the solar year, contains eighteen months of twenty days each, plus a terminal period, Uayeb, of five empty, or unlucky, days. The Tzolk is the sacred calendar of 260 days. These two calendars coincide only once every fifty-two years, on the Calendar Round. At those times, the Maya feared the end of the world, so priests performed religious ceremonies to prevent that from happening.

The Mayan calendar (pictured), developed thousands of years ago, was as accurate as the calendar used today.

Finally, the Long Count calendar measures longer periods of time, dating back to the mythical beginning of the Mayan era, a year they called 4-Ahau 8-Cumhu, or about 3111 B.C., when they believed the current universe was created. The Maya believed time extended backward and forward into infinity. Some carved stela mention dates almost 400 million years in the past.

The Maya did not see time as merely a means to record when events happened. To them, time had mystical significance. In their minds, a different god ruled over each era, and it was important to know which god to worship at the appropriate time.

CHAPTER FOUR

One God Above Many

Just as everyday life for the Maya was strictly controlled by their calendar, their lives were also ruled by complex religious beliefs. The calendar not only told them what to do each day but to which god to pray and make sacrifices. The Maya worshipped hundreds of gods in the heavens and on Earth. In their cities, buildings reflected their belief that mountains connected the earth to the heavens, and that caves were a link between Earth and the underworld. Pyramids were constructed to simulate mountains, and temple doorways represented caves.

For years, those who studied the Maya believed they had not practiced human sacrifice to appease their gods until late in their history. In 1946, with the discovery of the early Mayan center of Bonampak, these beliefs were disproved. According to murals and sculptures found there, the Maya, like the Aztec, practiced human sacrifice to appease their gods.

Mayan Religious Beliefs

Benevolent gods such as Chac, the rain god; Yum Kax, god of corn and agriculture; and Ixchel, goddess of floods, pregnancy, weaving, and the moon, helped the Maya in their daily lives. Not all Mayan gods were helpful, though. Yum Cimil was the primary god of death and ruled Mitnal, the ninth and lowest level of hell. To this

Opposite Page: Yum Kax, the maize god, was one of the hundreds of gods who controlled all aspects of Mayan life.

The Maya built structures and monuments, like this sculpture of the benevolent rain god Chac, to honor the deities.

day, Yucatán Maya believe Yum Cimil hovers near the sick, looking for victims.

In addition to the main gods, the Maya worshipped hundreds of minor gods. They believed every living thing had a spirit and that a god or goddess ruled over everything in nature. The following prayer, offered by a Maya worker to Huitz-Hok, or "Mountain-Valley," before he cut down a forest to prepare his field for sowing, was translated from a Mayan hieroglyph:

> O God, my mother, my father, Huitz-Hok, Lord Hills and Valleys, Che, Lord Forest, be patient with me, for I am about to do as my fathers have

ever done. . . . I am about to dirty you—to destroy your beauty—I am going to work you that I may obtain my daily bread. I pray you suffer no animal to attack me, nor snake to bite me. . . . Bid the trees that they fall not upon me, and suffer not the ax or knife to cut me, for with all my heart, I am about to work you.[2]

Belief in an Afterlife

The Maya not only believed in many gods, they also anticipated life after death. Their funeral rituals prove the existence of this belief. The Maya were not sure of the nature of life after death, but they did confess their sins before they died.

In the funeral rite of a Mayan nobleman, priests placed ground maize and jade beads in the corpse's mouth, and he was buried with most of his possessions. Priests filled pottery with food and drink to sustain the man's spirit during his journey to the other world. A nobleman was sometimes buried with other people, or dogs, so their spirits could guide him.

The Mayan concept of heaven included a place shaded by "the first tree of the world." Warriors killed

A funeral mask (pictured) sometimes rested on the face of a deceased king or noble. This practice and others reflected the Maya's strong belief in an afterlife.

The Myth of the Chanes

One of the most fascinating myths of the Maya is one that foretold the arrival of the Spanish conquistadors in the 1500s. This legend was common among pre–Columbian Indian civilizations in Mexico and Central America. It tells about the arrival of ships in the Gulf of Mexico of a race of fair-skinned men who eventually become leaders and rulers of the dark-skinned natives. This race of fair-skinned people was known as Chanes.

According to the legends, strange sea vessels appeared at the mouth of the Pánuco River, in the Mexican state of Tamaulipas. The sides of the vessels shone like serpents' scales, and the simple natives thought they were seeing great serpents swim-

A Mayan legend foretold the Spanish conquistadors' arrival by sea.

ming toward them. In the ships were light-skinned beings, whom some have said were tall and had blue eyes. They wore strange garments on their bodies and emblems like intertwined serpents on their foreheads. The natives of Mexico believed they were gods who had come to teach them and to guide them.

in battle, sacrificial victims, women who died in childbirth, and priests were thought to go there after death. The Maya also believed people who committed suicide by hanging would go to this special place when they died.

Religious Ceremonies

To keep the universe running as it should, and to prevent disasters or the end of the world, Mayan gods had to be kept happy. This was accomplished through religious ceremonies and often through sacrifices to feed the gods. When something bad happened—a drought or

The noblewoman depicted in this carving draws a thorn rope through her tongue to offer a blood sacrifice to the gods. Ku'l, *the blood of living things, was the most precious offering.*

flood, for example—it was thought to be the action of an angry god who felt neglected or insulted.

Religious rituals took place every day in peasant homes and on the steps of great stone temples. In Mayan huts, a mother offered bits of tortilla to Ixchel for the health of her child. A farmer, before beginning his chores, burned incense and prayed to Chac to bring rain to his fields. Some ceremonies involved offering food, tobacco, or alcoholic beverages to the gods. Others involved the most precious of offerings— life itself.

The sacred essence of life, what the Maya called *k'ul*, was the blood of living things. Offering *k'ul* to the gods was considered necessary on special occasions. The nature of the sacrifice depended on the importance of the event. The offering might be small birds, animals, or human blood. Among the Maya, human sacrifice was not a common occurrence as it was among the Aztec. Only major rituals, such as the coronation of a new ruler, a natural disaster, or the dedication of a new temple or ball court, required human victims.

Sometimes, brave individuals cut themselves to provide blood for the sacrifice. They often pierced their tongues and passed a rough cord through the hole to drain their blood onto a sacrificial stone. Parents sometimes offered sons or daughters to be sacrificed. These children were treated as royalty before the sacrifice. Then, they were either ritualistically killed by the priests, or they threw themselves into sacred wells to drown.

The Maya often offered captured prisoners, such as those in this fresco, as human sacrifices for the gods.

In many cases, captured prisoners became victims for human sacrifice. Some were bound, bent over a stone altar, and had their hearts removed. In 1566, Diego de Landa reported that another technique often used by the Maya was to have a large group of individuals fire arrows into the body of the sacrificial victim:

> The people went through a solemn dance . . . around the wooden pillar [where the victim was tied]. . . . [When] the . . . priest [made] a sign to the dancers, they began in order as they passed rapidly, dancing, to shoot an arrow to the victim's heart, . . . and quickly made of his chest a single point, like a hedgehog of arrows.[3]

The victim's blood was usually burned in a vessel on the temple steps. His body was then cut up and eaten by the priests and others attending the ceremony. Heads of decapitated victims were sometimes worn by Mayan kings as trophies or buried in the tombs of dead rulers.

The Maya sacrificed to the gods to bring them good fortune, but with the arrival of the Spanish, their luck ran out. One Mayan prophet quoted in the book *Chilam Balam of Chumayel*, foresaw the event, telling his people to "receive your guests, the bearded men, the men who come from the East. On that day, a blight is on the face of the earth." Elsewhere in the holy writings, though, is the admission that the Maya may have been as much to blame for their decline. "There were no more lucky days for us; we had no sound judgment."[4]

The Maya still live much as their ancestors did, but their empire is gone forever.

Notes

Chapter 2: Daily Life

1. Diego de Landa, "Yucatán Before and After the Conquest," from *Relación de las Cosas de Yucatán*, 1566, trans. William Gates. New York: Dover, 1978, p. 90.

Chapter 4: One God Above Many

2. Thomas Gann and J. Eric Thompson, *The History of the Maya*. New York: Charles Scribner's Sons, 1931, p. 123.
3. de Landa, "Yucatán Before and After the Conquest," p. 48.
4. Quoted in Editors of Time-Life Books, *The Magnificent Maya*. Alexandria, VA: Time-Life, 1993, p. 150.

Glossary

artifact: An object made or changed by humans, especially a tool or weapon used in the past.

astrology: The study of how the positions of the stars and planets supposedly affect people's lives.

cenote: Spanish word for a natural well, formed when the ground gives way and falls into an underground water supply.

conquistador: A Spanish soldier and adventurer, part of the Spanish expedition to the New World in the 1500s.

hieroglyphics: Writing used by ancient civilizations, made up of pictures and symbols.

mural: A painting on a wall.

obsidian: A dark, glassy volcanic rock.

pagan: Someone who is not a member of the Christian, Jewish, or Muslim religion. A pagan may worship many gods or have no religion at all.

rain forest: A dense forest that receives a lot of rain.

stela: Upright slabs or pillars, usually of stone, inscribed with carvings or writing.

thatched roof: A roof made from straw or reeds.

For More Information

Books

Elizabeth Baquedano, *Eyewitness: Aztec, Inca, and Maya.* New York: DK, 2000.

Laurie Coulter, *Secrets in Stone: All About Maya Hieroglyphics.* New York: Little, Brown Children's Books, 2001.

Judith Crosher, *Technology in the Time of the Maya.* New York: Raintree, 1998.

Tami Deedrick, *Maya.* New York: Raintree, 2001.

Websites

Jaguar Sun
(www.jaguar-sun.com)
A site created by the author of a historically accurate novel about the Maya, containing her research on Mayan culture, the Maya today, and the ancient civilization. Well researched and easy to navigate.

Maya Ruins.com
(www.mayaruins.com)
A site with fascinating interactive maps of the ruins of major Mayan cities and lots of on-site photographs.

Mundo Maya Online

(www.mayadiscovery.com)

The online magazine *Mundo Maya*, or *the Maya World*. Information in English and Spanish about the history, geography, daily life, and art of the Maya. Archived articles, with plenty of photos.

Mystery of the Maya

(www.civilization.ca)

A site to accompany the Imax film *Mystery of the Maya*. Plenty of information, links, and photos. Easy to navigate. Maintained by the Canadian Museum of Civilization.

Index

Picture Credits

About the Author

Charles and Linda George have written more than forty nonfiction books for children and teens. Their books include *Texas, The Sioux, The Comanche, The Holocaust, Plate Tectonics,* and *Uranus* for KidHaven Press, and *Gene Therapy* for Blackbirch Press. They both taught in Texas public schools before retiring to write full time. Charles taught secondary history and Spanish, and Linda taught in the elementary grades. They live in the mountains of New Mexico.